Original title:
The Glow of Longing

Copyright © 2025 Swan Charm
All rights reserved.

Author: Sabrina Sarvik
ISBN HARDBACK: 978-9908-1-4999-8
ISBN PAPERBACK: 978-9908-1-5000-0
ISBN EBOOK: 978-9908-1-5001-7

Luminous Echoes in Sweet Solitude

In whispers soft, the twilight sings,
A dance of light on fragile wings.
Each shadow bows to golden gleam,
In gentle night, we find our dream.

The stars awake, a silent choir,
Their twinkling notes, a soothing fire.
In quietude, the heart expands,
To hear the song of distant lands.

Beneath the moon's serene embrace,
We wander forth in tranquil grace.
With every step, a tale unfolds,
In silver threads, the night beholds.

Echoes of laughter, soft and wide,
In sweet solitude, we confide.
The world outside fades into night,
As dreams take wing in soft moonlight.

In this realm, the spirit soars,
Unlocking hearts and opening doors.
With luminous echoes, we unite,
In sweet solitude, all feels right.

Embracing Dusk's Warmth

In the hush of the fading light,
Shadows dance, both soft and slight.
Hearts entwined in whispered dreams,
As daylight fades, and silence gleams.

Waves of warmth brush past our skin,
The world exhales, where we begin.
Golden hues wrap 'round the trees,
In this moment, time does freeze.

Stars peek through as dusk unfolds,
Stories lingering, yet untold.
With every breath, the night draws near,
Embracing dusk, we lose our fear.

A gentle breeze caresses us,
In silence shared, there's no rush.
Hand in hand, we wander slow,
Discovering what we both know.

Endless skies and vibrant tones,
In twilight's arms, we make our homes.
Together here, we'll find our way,
Through the magic of this day.

Flashes of Eclipsed Speech

In shadows cast by fleeting light,
Words suppressed, yet feels so right.
Every glance a silent plea,
As moments pass, just you and me.

Through the veil of twilight's hue,
Unspoken truths ignite the view.
Secret languages intertwined,
In this dance, our hearts aligned.

The silence hums, a vibrant thread,
In hesitant whispers, truths are spread.
Each pause is a verse, softly spun,
As echoes linger, two become one.

Eclipsed thoughts, like stars, appear,
In the stillness, we draw near.
A glimpse of worlds we've yet to speak,
Where love's the language, soft and sleek.

Beneath the moon, with hearts ablaze,
We find connection in a maze.
Each flash a spark, igniting the soul,
In eclipsed speech, we feel the whole.

Unfinished Stories in the Glow

In the twilight, tales unfold,
Of secrets kept and dreams retold.
Pages unwritten, ink still wet,
A promise made we won't forget.

Frayed edges of stories to weave,
With every breath, we dare believe.
The glow casts shadows on the wall,
In unison, we stand tall.

Moments linger, the night is young,
Melodies of hopes unsung.
Each whisper holds a hidden quest,
In the silence, we're truly blessed.

Underneath this starry shroud,
We write our tales, fierce and loud.
Unfinished stories, hearts in sync,
In vibrant colors, we truly think.

As dawn approaches, dreams ignite,
These fragments dance, a beautiful sight.
Together we'll pen our endless scrolls,
In the glow of night, we find our roles.

Glimpses of a Fading Horizon

At the edge where sky meets sea,
Glimpses dance, wild and free.
Horizon whispers, fading light,
Promises sewn into the night.

Colors blend in soft embrace,
Every wave, a fleeting trace.
Moments blend with fading sighs,
In every glance, a new surprise.

As time drifts on, we stand still,
Caught in beauty, against our will.
Horizons stretch beyond our grasp,
Yet in this moment, life's a clasp.

With every tide that ebbs and flows,
In the twilight, our love grows.
Chasing dreams through shadows thin,
We find our way where hopes begin.

Each sunset holds our whispered grace,
In fading light, we find our place.
Together facing the unknown,
In glimpses of forever shown.

Twilight's Gentle Embrace

The sun dips low, a whispered sigh,
Shadows stretch across the sky.
Stars begin to twinkle bright,
In the arms of coming night.

Soft breezes hum a tender tune,
Under the gaze of the sleepy moon.
Daylight fades, a soft retreat,
Embraced by dusk, serene and sweet.

Light-Drenched Memories

Golden rays through windows pour,
Illuminating what we adore.
Moments captured, sweet and dear,
Echoes of laughter draw us near.

Pages turn in a sunbeam's glow,
Stories shared, fond memories flow.
In every smile and gentle glance,
Time stands still in a fleeting dance.

Unfolding in Soft Light

Petals bloom in morning's grace,
Each one holds a story's trace.
Sunlight spills on dew-kissed ground,
Whispered secrets can be found.

Nature hums a gentle rhyme,
In this moment, we transcend time.
As day unfolds, dreams take flight,
Cradled softly in morning light.

Illuminated by What Lies Ahead

A path unwinds, both bright and clear,
Filled with hope, devoid of fear.
Footsteps echo in twilight's glow,
Guiding us where we must go.

With each turn, new joys arise,
Beneath the vast, embracing skies.
Futures shine like stars above,
Leading us forth with endless love.

Whispers in the Twilight

The sun has dipped beyond the hill,
Shadows dance with silent thrill.
A gentle breeze carries a sigh,
As nightfall paints the endless sky.

Stars awaken, twinkling bright,
Guardians of the velvet night.
They whisper secrets, soft and low,
Of dreams forgotten long ago.

Moonlight spills on leaves and grass,
Time, it slows, as moments pass.
Wrapped in twilight's tender glow,
Hearts can find a way to flow.

A hush descends, the world holds breath,
In this stillness, silence wraps flesh.
Every whisper, a soft embrace,
In twilight's arms, we find our place.

So linger here, let shadows roam,
For in this quiet, we find home.
Whispers linger, soft and true,
In twilight's glow, just me and you.

Flickers of Desire

In the dusk, embers ignite,
Flickers dance, a wild flight.
Passions swell, hearts entwine,
In every glance, a spark divine.

Golden hues laced with dreams,
Starlit paths and silent screams.
Hopes ignite with every beat,
In this fire, our souls meet.

With every whisper, desires grow,
In shadows deep, our love can flow.
Cinders glow beneath the night,
Flickers hint the purest light.

Holding tight through flame and fear,
Every flicker draws you near.
In the dark, where shadows play,
Love's sweet whispers, come what may.

Embers pulse with fierce delight,
An endless dance, a pure invite.
Flickers of desire, burning bright,
Together lost in the velvet night.

Ember Hearts Embrace

In the glow of a fading light,
Two ember hearts hold on tight.
Whispers soft, a tender trace,
In the night, they find their grace.

Fires of passion gently blaze,
In silent nights, the heart conveys.
Every heartbeat a sweet refrain,
In each other, they find their gain.

Through the stillness, dreams arise,
Wrapped in hope beneath the skies.
Ember hearts, they softly weave,
A tapestry of love, believe.

Moments spark like glowing ash,
Time stands still, the shadows clash.
In this embrace, they feel alive,
Two ember hearts that always thrive.

As the world fades into night,
Embers glow, a soft delight.
Together in this fevered space,
Two souls bound in love's embrace.

Yearning in the Starlight

Underneath the starlit dome,
Yearning hearts find their home.
Moonlight spills on whispered dreams,
As love flows in soft moonbeams.

In the night, desires rise,
Painted by the velvet skies.
Each twinkle holds a secret plea,
In this space, just you and me.

Every star a distant fire,
Awakening our hidden desire.
With every wish upon the night,
We explore love's pure delight.

Yearning calls like a lover's song,
A sweet echo where we belong.
In the stillness, hearts take flight,
Yearning deep in the starlight.

With twilight's glow, let dreams unfold,
In our hearts, a story told.
Yearning whispers in the dark,
Guided by love's eternal spark.

Soft Sparks of Distant Longing

In twilight's gentle embrace,
Whispers dance through the air,
Soft sparks ignite the night,
Craving warmth, tender and rare.

Stars flutter like lost thoughts,
Casting dreams on silken skies,
Each one a wish unspoken,
Beneath the moon's watchful eyes.

Shadows weave through the silence,
Holding secrets of the heart,
Yearning for a distant spark,
Where love and distance part.

Time flows, a river of hope,
Carrying echoes of sighs,
Mapping out the depth of longing,
In the realm where passion lies.

Dance of fireflies, so fleeting,
Illuminate the darkened night,
Guiding hearts to find their way,
In the soft, enchanting light.

Luminescent Pathways of Desire

Beneath the canopy of stars,
We stroll on pathways of dreams,
Each step a flicker of longing,
Materialized in moonbeams.

Winds whisper sweet nothings,
As petals fall like soft rain,
Tracing lines of desire,
In the heart, a tender pain.

Every glance holds a promise,
Every touch ignites a spark,
In the silence, we find solace,
As darkness wraps us in its arc.

Adjacent hearts like rivers flow,
Connecting in a silent plea,
Luminescent trails of yearning,
Carved in moonlit reverie.

The night's rhythm calls our names,
Underneath the vast expanse,
In this dance of love and longing,
We surrender to the chance.

Shadows Stretching towards Dreams

In the garden of the night,
Shadows stretch and intertwine,
Seeking solace in twilight,
Reaching for a love divine.

Whispers drift on gentle winds,
Carrying tales of the heart,
In each breeze, a hope ascends,
Promising we'll never part.

Starlit paths that lead us on,
Through the valleys of our minds,
Where the echoes of our dreams,
In each other, we will find.

Tangled roots of longing grow,
In the soil of our desire,
Together we will brave the storm,
Fanning faith into a fire.

As dawn breaks with sweet closure,
Casting light on shadows' seam,
We emerge from night's embrace,
To heed the call of our dream.

Celestial Whispers of Longing

In the quiet of twilight hours,
Celestial whispers weave the air,
Woven tales of distant stars,
Unraveling the spaces we share.

Each sigh carries fragrant dreams,
Sweet notes of yearning softly rise,
Painting our souls with desire,
Under the canvas of endless skies.

Time suspended in this moment,
Fingers lost in silken threads,
Every heartbeat syncs with echoes,
Of the dreams that dance in our heads.

Through silent prayers and wishes,
We chart a course on love's vast sea,
Where hope unfurls like starlit sails,
Blessed by the light of destiny.

In this realm of whispered longing,
We find refuge in each other's eyes,
As celestial wonders align,
Uniting hearts beneath the skies.

A Distance Wrapped in Light

In twilight's glow, the stars appear,
Whispers of dreams, fading yet near.
Shadows that dance on the edges of night,
A distance embraced in the softest light.

Waves of the cosmos, a gentle sweep,
Secrets held close, in silence they keep.
The universe hums, a ethereal tune,
As light stretches forth like a silver moon.

Beyond the horizon, where hopes reside,
In the arms of the dawn, we often confide.
A journey unfolds with each step we take,
Wrapped in the light, no fear left to wake.

Moments like dew, fragile yet bold,
Carried on whispers, each story told.
The distance now brief, as hearts intertwine,
In a tapestry woven of starlight divine.

Radiant Echoes of the Past

In the corners of memory, shadows collide,
Radiant echoes, a time-traveling ride.
A laughter that lingers, a tear that will trace,
The light of the present, the past's warm embrace.

Woven with threads of laughter and pain,
Through seasons of sunshine and moments of rain.
Whispers of ages, in soft twilight's call,
Radiant echoes of all, stand proud and tall.

In faces remembered, in songs that we sing,
The fabric of life, with all that it brings.
Each heartbeat a ledger, each breath a new chance,
To dance with the past in a timeless romance.

Through echoes of voices, the lessons resound,
In the still of the night, such solace is found.
With luminous heartbeats, we carry it on,
The radiant whispers of all who have gone.

The Warmth of Hidden Cravings

Beneath the surface, where desires reside,
The warmth of hidden cravings can't hide.
A flicker, a flame, in the hush of the night,
Longing ignites with soft whispers of light.

Moments of silence that beckon the dream,
Lost in the shadows, where passions redeem.
Each heartbeat a rhythm, a dance in disguise,
The warmth rises slow with each glance of the eyes.

In secretive gardens where wishes might grow,
Beneath the soft moon, the desires will show.
As sweetness unfolds in the breath of the air,
The warmth of cravings, a truth we must share.

Wrapped in the stillness, a sanctuary fine,
Imagining worlds, where souls intertwine.
With every desire, a spark to ignite,
The warmth of longing envelops the night.

Fireside Secrets of the Soul

By the flicker of flames, stories unfold,
Fireside secrets of warmth, yet untold.
Each ember glowing, a heart's silent plea,
In the dance of the fire, souls whisper and see.

Memories linger, with shadows that sway,
In the circle of warmth, we find our own way.
The crackle of wood holds the weight of our fears,
Fireside confessions, igniting the tears.

With each spark that soars, we rise from the cold,
A tapestry woven with threads of the bold.
The quiet reflections, a solace so deep,
In the heart of the fire, our secrets we keep.

In laughter and stories, our lives intertwined,
Fireside whispers, leaving none behind.
The glow of the hearth, a sanctuary sweet,
Fireside secrets of the soul, feel complete.

Halos of Heartfelt Longing

In the quiet night they glow,
Soft whispers weave through the air.
Fingers stretch to touch the light,
Chasing dreams beyond compare.

Every heartbeat sways like trees,
With gentle winds that call my name.
Each moment holds a secret note,
In the symphony of love's game.

Clouds drift slowly, painted pale,
Brushing hues of molten gold.
Every glance is a silent prayer,
A story waiting to be told.

Time dances lightly, fleeting grace,
While stars in their wisdom gleam.
In the shadows, hope finds form,
Breathing life into our dream.

As dawn awakens, hearts ignite,
The fire of longing always burns.
In every tear, a promise shines,
For love, it endlessly returns.

Phantoms of Luminous Yearning

In the twilight's gentle fold,
Memories linger, soft and sweet.
Whispers echo in the dark,
Each sigh a bittersweet retreat.

Figures dance in the silver glow,
Casting shadows, shapes entwined.
A melody lost, yet profound,
In the chambers of the mind.

Longing wraps around each dream,
Like moonlight on a restless sea.
Phantoms hum a haunting tune,
Singing truths we choose to see.

Waves of time flow endlessly,
Each heartbeat drips like dew.
In the silence, secrets stir,
A world framed just for two.

Through the dusk, a lantern glows,
Guiding hearts into the vast.
And though we chase what is elusive,
Together, we shall hold fast.

Beacons in the Fading Dusk

Amidst the dusk, soft lights arise,
Whispers calling from afar.
Hope flickers like the distant stars,
A promise sealed beneath the scar.

Each heartbeat echoes in the dark,
As shadows dance on ages past.
Every glance a fleeting spark,
In dreams that glow, they ever last.

Beacons rise on the path we tread,
Illuminating what's unseen.
In the fading light we forge ahead,
With love to guide, our hearts serene.

Through valleys deep and mountains high,
Together, souls entwine their fate.
In every step, a silent vow,
With every dawn, we recreate.

Fading dusk becomes our muse,
As twilight wraps us in its grace.
In the soft embrace, we'll choose,
To be each other's warmest place.

Wickedly Beautiful Longing

In the garden of untamed dreams,
Desire blooms with petals bright.
Each glance a thorn, yet soft it seems,
Entangled in a velvet night.

Laughter dances on the breeze,
Wicked whispers through the leaves.
Behind closed eyes, we tease the flames,
In every word, the heart believes.

Beautiful chaos wraps around,
Crimson threads in moonlit seams.
In the dark, our shadows bound,
Breeding life into our dreams.

Every heartbeat drums in time,
With the secrets that we keep.
Wickedly woven, souls entwined,
In the silence, we'll not sleep.

Longing lingers, sweet and wild,
Like the tempest's fervent song.
In each heartbeat, I am beguiled,
Wickedly, where we belong.

Unreachable Rays of Light

Golden hues stretch far and wide,
Casting warmth where shadows hide.
A dance of hope in the sky,
Yet just beyond, they seem to fly.

Silent whispers call my name,
In every glow, a fleeting flame.
Though I reach with open hands,
They shimmer softly, like distant sands.

Time slips by, and dreams grow bold,
Moments gleam, yet never hold.
In aching hearts, we chase and yearn,
For every radiance we discern.

Each dawn, I rise to face the chase,
Finding beauty in every trace.
While unreachable, they still inspire,
Filling souls with vibrant fire.

So I'll wander, eyes set high,
With every glance toward the sky.
For even as the distance stays,
I'll keep seeking those bright rays.

Whispered Wishes on the Breeze

Softly spoken, secrets shared,
Carried gently, showing we cared.
In the night, a tender sigh,
Wishes floating, soaring high.

Through the trees, a gentle song,
Echoing where hearts belong.
Every wish on the wind's soft flight,
Brings us hope in the fading light.

As the stars blink in delight,
We find solace in the night.
Each whisper holds a dream reborn,
In the silence, new paths are worn.

Breezes soothe our restless hearts,
Guiding us as the journey starts.
In their song, we find our peace,
With every wish, our fears release.

Together, we'll share our dreams,
In the hush, nothing's as it seems.
With whispers carried on the night,
Our hearts entwined, we take flight.

Flickers of Everlasting Dreams

In the stillness of the dawn,
Flickers rise, hope's gentle spawn.
Dreams ignite in amber light,
Guided softly, shining bright.

Each heartbeat fuels the sacred flame,
A dance of wishes, never the same.
In every soul, a spark concealed,
Awaiting time to be revealed.

Through the storms and through the strife,
We nurture dreams, embracing life.
With every flicker, shadows flee,
In the glow, we find our plea.

Moments crafted, strands entwined,
In these dreams, our hearts aligned.
For as we soar, we'll never fade,
In the light, our journeys made.

So let us chase the flickering gleam,
Wrapped in hope, alive in dream.
With every breath, we rise anew,
In everlasting dreams, we grew.

Radiant Threads of Connection

In a world full of silent cries,
Radiant threads weave through the skies.
Each heartbeat and every glance,
Connects us in a timeless dance.

Invisible bonds through space and time,
We hold each other, hearts in rhyme.
In laughter shared, in tears we shed,
These radiant threads forever spread.

From whispering pines to city lights,
Our stories merge, igniting nights.
In every soul, a story spun,
As we journey, we become one.

So let us cherish every tie,
In the brightness, we learn to fly.
With every thread that we create,
Connection's warmth will never wait.

Together we weave this tapestry,
A vision strong, a grand decree.
In the fabric of our dreams, we find,
Radiant threads where love is blind.

Ripples of Pained Anticipation

The clock ticks slow, a heavy sound,
A heart in wait, where hope is drowned.
Fingers twitch with dreams unspun,
Each moment stretched, a battle won.

Shadows creep where light once danced,
A silent scream for a fleeting chance.
Yet in the depths, a whisper grows,
Through muted pain, a fire glows.

Waves of doubt crash on the shore,
But still we yearn, we seek for more.
Each breath a step through tangled fear,
In shadows cast, our dreams draw near.

Branches tremble with gentle sighs,
Beneath the weight of uncried cries.
The soul's canvas, streaked with gray,
But colors wait to find their way.

A quiet moment, a final plea,
In starlit skies, we yearn to see.
For in the silence, promise waits,
Beyond the pain, the heart creates.

Cascade of Glimmers Unseen

In twilight's grasp, the day departs,
While night unveils its secret arts.
Whispers dance on gentle streams,
Painting shadows, haunting dreams.

A shimmer caught in silken webs,
Each droplet holds a dream that ebbs.
Beneath the moon, the world feels wide,
An ocean of hope, where hearts collide.

Fleeting glances, a spark ignites,
Drawing souls through the endless nights.
Soft echoes of laughter, untamed,
In the cascade, their joy is framed.

Stars cascade in a velvet sea,
Guiding hearts with a tender plea.
For in the depths of the unseen,
Lie treasures that have always been.

A journey started with a sigh,
In the silence, dreams do lie.
Through whispered wishes, two become one,
In cascading light, they greet the dawn.

The Dance of Light and Shadow

Amidst the dusk, they start to sway,
Both light and dark, in bright array.
A waltz of whispers in the night,
Creating softness, blurring sight.

Shadowed corners, secrets kept,
In every twirl, a promise wept.
They beckon forth, a silent call,
As silhouettes rise, softly fall.

Flickering flames in the bittersweet,
Filling the air with rhythmic beat.
Each pulse of light, a tender grace,
Tracing patterns in empty space.

Beneath the stars, they weave a tale,
Of hopes and dreams that seldom pale.
A moment caught, a memory spun,
In every heartbeat, two become one.

As dawn breaks forth, they gently part,
Yet forever etched within the heart.
For in their dance, the world seems whole,
An endless waltz of heart and soul.

Tidal Waves of Forgotten Joys

Where echoes linger, the past holds tight,
In waves of laughter, lost in light.
Memories crash against the shore,
Tidal pulls that we can't ignore.

Amidst the foam, a glimpse appears,
Of childish dreams, of uncried tears.
Fragments flutter on breezes lost,
Reminders of a forgotten cost.

The ocean depth, a keeper's vault,
Hiding treasures, no one would fault.
Yet every surge brings forth a song,
A melody where we belong.

In twilight's hue, as stars ignite,
We chase reflections in the night.
For even in the darkest tides,
The heart's joy pulls, and hope abides.

Through shifting sands, we find our way,
In every wave, our hearts convey.
For in the rush of life's embrace,
Lie dormant joys that time can't erase.

Twilight's Dance of Desire

In the soft glow of fading light,
Whispers of longing take to flight.
Stars awaken in the deepening sky,
As shadows embrace, hearts draw nigh.

A secret glance, a breathless pause,
Every heartbeat, a silent cause.
Moved by the lure of fading day,
Two souls entwined, lost in play.

With each moment, passion ignites,
In the dance of dusk, dreams take flight.
The world fades away, just we remain,
In twilight's glow, love's sweet refrain.

Tender Rays of Atonement

Morning breaks with gentle grace,
Soft light spills, a warm embrace.
Forgiveness blooms in the sun's bright glow,
As shadows of doubt begin to slow.

Each ray speaks of hopes renewed,
Of healing pains and love pursued.
In the stillness, hearts conspire,
To rise above, to mend, to inspire.

Through tender whispers, we begin,
To let the light shine from within.
Embracing warmth, we step outside,
In tender rays, our truth won't hide.

Veils of Soft Light

As dusk descends, veils gently fall,
Shrouded wonders, a siren's call.
Mysterious paths beneath the moon,
Where shadows dance, revealing tunes.

A tender breeze stirs the night,
Carrying dreams, taking flight.
In soft light's embrace, we find our way,
Through veils of silence, we choose to stay.

Revelations bloom in the pale glow,
Secrets spun in the night's flow.
Within the veils, we lose our fears,
And weave together hopes and tears.

Footsteps in the Dimming Radiance

Where daylight fades and shadows creep,
Footprints linger, memories keep.
In twilight's hush, stories unfold,
Of journeys taken and dreams retold.

Each step echoes on paths we've tread,
In the soft warmth of what lies ahead.
With every heartbeat, time intertwines,
In dimming radiance, love aligns.

As night unfurls its starry cloak,
We whisper promises, softly spoke.
In the fleeting glow, we hold on tight,
Guided by love through the quiet night.

Whispers of a Distant Star

In the night sky so wide and clear,
A twinkling light, a voice we hear.
Softly calling from realms afar,
Promises held by a distant star.

Mysteries wrapped in velvet dark,
Each glimmer sings, ignites a spark.
Stories woven through time and space,
In the silence, we find our place.

The cosmos dances, a silent tune,
Guiding our hearts, like the phases of moon.
In stillness, the whispers flow and part,
Echoes of dreams that dwell in the heart.

Through the vastness, we search and roam,
In that light, we feel at home.
Yearning souls, drawn by the night,
Captured forever in starlit flight.

So let us listen, let us believe,
In the gentle whispers, we shall receive.
For in the darkness, hope's light will spar,
Guided by whispers of a distant star.

Ember Hues of Desire

In the glow of the fading light,
Embers dance in the soft night.
Crimson and gold, a fiery kiss,
In every spark, a moment of bliss.

With every flicker, dreams take flight,
Whispers of passion in the dark night.
Craving warmth, in shadows we play,
Lost in the warmth, we drift away.

Eager hearts, in yearning's embrace,
Caught in a deep, enchanting space.
Fires of longing, they burn so bright,
Guiding our souls to the edge of night.

In ember hues, we find our song,
A melody where we both belong.
With every breath, our desires ignite,
In this dance, we write our own light.

As the night deepens, passions swell,
In the heat of dreams, we weave our spell.
Hold me close, let the embers inspire,
Forever lost in this ember of desire.

Echoes in the Twilight

Twilight whispers through the trees,
Softly swaying in the breeze.
Shadows lengthen, time stands still,
Echoes call, our hearts they fill.

The world bathed in a tender glow,
Memories drift like falling snow.
In this moment, silence sings,
Carried on winds, gentle wings.

Stars awaken in the dusky veil,
Stories of love begin to unveil.
In shadows deep, secrets reside,
In twilight's arms, we will confide.

So let us linger, hold this view,
As day fades to night, what's old feels new.
Under the sky painted in hue,
We find ourselves lost in the true.

Echoes linger, a sweet refrain,
In the twilight's grace, we feel no pain.
Together we dance, hearts intertwined,
In whispers of time, forever enshrined.

Lanterns in the Heart

In the quiet of night, lanterns gleam,
Flickering softly, they light up our dream.
Each glowing orb holds a secret wish,
A tender thought, a yearning's kiss.

When shadows creep, and doubts arise,
Lanterns shine bright, igniting the skies.
Through darkened paths, they guide our way,
Leading us home, where love will stay.

With every beat, our hearts align,
Illuminated by love's design.
In the soft glow, we dare to start,
A journey bound by lanterns in the heart.

As the night deepens, dreams take flight,
With lanterns as beacons in the night.
Together we wander, hand in hand,
In this glow, we understand.

So let the lanterns guide us near,
Filling the world with hope and cheer.
For in their light, we find our part,
Together forever, lanterns in the heart.

Light as a Feather

In the morning light so bright,
Feathers dance on sudden flight.
Whispers float on gentle breeze,
Carrying dreams with graceful ease.

Through the trees, they weave and sway,
Softly guiding where they play.
In the skies, they find their place,
Drifting lightly, full of grace.

Hope takes wing in every heart,
A chance to rise, to love, to start.
Together lifted, spirits soar,
Free like feathers, forevermore.

With every turn, a tale unfolds,
Of love and laughter yet untold.
In vibrant hues of sunset's glow,
Light as a feather, free we flow.

Heart as a Stone

In the shadows, cold and gray,
Lies a heart that's lost its way.
Chiseled edges, sharp and rough,
In silence echoes, I am tough.

Walls built high, but life still calls,
Brick and mortar, nothing small.
Heavy burdens weigh me down,
In the stillness, I can drown.

Yet beneath this hardened shell,
A flicker of warmth, a secret well.
Yearning deep for light to break,
To shift the stone and mend the ache.

If I could just let feelings flow,
Release the weight, let softness grow.
To transform this heart of stone,
Into a home, no more alone.

Shimmering Threads of Fate

In the silence of the night,
Threads of silver gleam in sight.
Weaving stories intertwined,
With each twist, our fates aligned.

Across the stars, connections spark,
Lighting pathways in the dark.
Every choice a thread we weave,
In the tapestry we believe.

In delicate hands, the threads reside,
Carried by the turning tide.
Moments passed and futures cast,
Each whisper binding, holding fast.

With every heartbeat, paths collide,
Guiding us where dreams abide.
In shimmering hues of chance and fate,
We find our truth, we learn to wait.

Lanterns of Unclaimed Affection

Beneath the moon, they softly glow,
Lanterns hang in rows, a show.
Flickering lights of feelings untold,
In their warmth, hearts unfold.

Unclaimed whispers in the air,
Hints of longing linger there.
Softly calling, drawing near,
With every pulse, the hope is clear.

A tender glance ignites the flame,
In shared silence, no one's name.
Hearts align, yet still apart,
Guided by the unclaimed heart.

Through the night, we wander slow,
Seeking truths in the soft glow.
Holding dreams in shadows low,
Lanterns guide us where to go.

Heartbeats in the Half-Light

In the dusky twilight's embrace,
Heartbeat whispers, a secret place.
Soft and steady, the rhythm calls,
Echoing where the darkness falls.

Each moment floats, a fleeting sigh,
Colors blend in a gentle sky.
Fragile feelings courageously bloom,
As shadows dance and deepen the gloom.

With each heartbeat, we draw near,
In half-light's charm, we lose our fear.
Bound by silence, yet so alive,
In this space, our spirits thrive.

Beyond the veil, a world awaits,
Where love can build and dreams create.
Heartbeats linger, in sweet twilight,
Together we shine, a guiding light.

Radiance of Untold Wishes

In the twilight glow, dreams arise,
Soft whispers carried by the skies.
Each wish like a star, a flickering light,
Unfolding magic in the night.

In the garden of hopes, blooms so rare,
Heartbeats echo, drifting in air.
With every sigh, new stories weave,
A tapestry of what we believe.

Through the silence, solace is found,
In the depths where love is unbound.
Radiance flows, casting its spell,
In the quiet, our secrets dwell.

Flickering candles in the dark,
Guiding us with their tender spark.
Untold wishes gently unfurl,
Creating wonder in our world.

Embers dance, igniting the night,
Every hope a celestial flight.
In the dreamer's heart, a flicker grows,
Illuminating paths where love flows.

Heartstrings in Radiant Silence

In the silence where shadows play,
Heartstrings whisper, night turns to day.
Gentle echoes of dreams take flight,
Caressing souls with their light.

Every heartbeat sings a tune,
Underneath the watchful moon.
In this moment, time stands still,
We find solace, we find will.

Moments woven, soft and bright,
Radiant whispers fill the night.
Threads of connection, pure and true,
Drawing me closer, me to you.

As we linger in the quiet glow,
Secrets danced, only we know.
Every glance, a silent plea,
In this magic, we are free.

Together, hearts beat as one,
In the calm before the run.
Radiant silence holds us tight,
Guiding love through the night.

Threads of Distant Light

In the fabric of night, stars align,
Threads of light in a pattern divine.
Each flicker tells tales of old,
Whispers of warmth, a sight to behold.

Through the cosmos, journeys unfold,
Dreams intertwined in silver and gold.
Every thread a story shared,
In the universe, we're fully paired.

With every heartbeat, we reach high,
Grasping the wonders that fill the sky.
Boundless connections in the vast space,
In every twinkle, a familiar face.

As the night deepens, shadows grow,
Weaving our paths in the radiant glow.
Together we dance, together we shine,
In the tapestry of life, purely divine.

Threads of distant light unite,
Drawing us closer, hearts taking flight.
In this cosmic embrace, we belong,
Guided by love, forever strong.

Lanterns for the Unreachable

In the dusk, lanterns gleam bright,
Guiding souls through the endless night.
Each flickering flame, a wish cast free,
Lighting the way for you and me.

Through the haze, we chase our dreams,
Hope ignited by the soft beams.
In the stillness, we raise our gaze,
Wonders unfold in a shimmering haze.

Lanterns carried on the night wind,
A gentle reminder of where we've been.
Illuminating paths of the unknown,
With every flicker, our spirits have grown.

Through the darkness, courage flows,
A dance of visions that brightly glows.
Endless possibilities lie in wait,
Under stars that we cultivate.

Together we journey, hand in hand,
Across the shores of this dreamland.
Lanterns guiding us, hearts ablaze,
In this adventure, love always stays.

Celestial Yearning

Beneath the stars, I long to roam,
To touch the skies, to find my home.
In dreams I chase the moonlit glow,
As whispers of my heart bestow.

In cosmic dance, the galaxies spin,
I seek the light that dwells within.
With every breath, I call your name,
In stardust trails, I feel the flame.

The constellations hear my plea,
A universe that cradles me.
For love that stretches far and wide,
In every twinkle, you abide.

Each comet's flight, a vow to keep,
While night unfolds, it's you I seek.
In quiet moments, hearts entwined,
In celestial realms, our souls aligned.

As dawn approaches, dreams take flight,
A new horizon, painted bright.
Yet in my heart, the stars will stay,
Guiding my love, come what may.

The Radiance of Silent Wishes

In the hush of night, wishes bloom,
Softly glowing, dispelling gloom.
A whispered hope on the cool night air,
Promises linger, silent yet rare.

Beneath the stars, dreams softly glide,
Carried gently on the ebbing tide.
Each flicker speaks of desires held,
In the quiet where secrets meld.

A lantern's glow, a beacon true,
Illuminating paths meant for two.
In tranquil spaces where hearts align,
Radiant moments, forever shine.

The nightingale's song, a tender grace,
Echoes softly in this sacred place.
With every note, wishes ascend,
In the silence, our hearts blend.

As dawn arrives, wishes take flight,
Transforming dreams into daylight.
Though silent, the wishes abide,
In the warmth of love's embrace, side by side.

Flickering Shadows of Affection

In twilight's glow, shadows play,
Ebbing softly at the end of day.
With every flicker, love's warmth grows,
In the dance of dusk, our hearts compose.

Beneath the trees, whispers entwine,
In gentle breezes, our souls align.
Each shadow speaks of memories shared,
In silent moments, we have dared.

Lost in the flicker, time stands still,
In the soft embrace, we feel the thrill.
With soft caress of the moon's pale light,
Our hearts ignite, chasing the night.

A tapestry woven with threads of gold,
In shadows that flicker, our stories told.
Each echo of laughter, a tender trace,
Leaves a mark in this sacred space.

As the stars emerge, we hold on tight,
Flickering shadows in the still of night.
In love's embrace, we find our way,
Guided by the light that never frays.

Glistening Paths of Memory

On winding roads where memories gleam,
Each step we take is stitched in dream.
With glistening moments, we walk side by side,
In the heart's journal where love resides.

Through sunlit days and soft moonlight,
Our stories twinkle, pure delight.
In echoes of laughter, a melody plays,
A symphony cherished in countless ways.

In every glance, a tale bestowed,
Glistening paths on this shared road.
Whispers of time in delicate rhyme,
A treasure of moments that bloom in chime.

As seasons change, these memories flow,
In the tapestry of life, love will glow.
With every heartbeat, our journey reflects,
In glistening paths, our love connects.

Through each sunset, as shadows unfold,
We gather the stories that remain untold.
Together we wander, hand in hand free,
In glistening paths of memory.

Echoes of Unseen Dreams

In the quiet night, whispers call,
Faint murmurs rise, shadows fall.
Hopes like stars that dimly gleam,
Dancing softly, lost in dream.

Voices carried on the breeze,
Each note lingers, time to seize.
Fragments of light in the dark,
A canvas painted, a vivid spark.

Beneath the moon's gentle gaze,
They twirl in a delicate haze.
Where visions wander and souls unite,
In the corners of the night.

Memories brush against the skin,
Reminding us where we have been.
With every heartbeat, truth comes near,
Echoes of dreams we hold dear.

Let us embrace what lingers still,
The promise of tomorrow's thrill.
In the silence, love will beam,
Wrapped in echoes, unseen dream.

Luminous Shadows of Hope

In the twilight where shadows play,
Gentle light finds its way.
Hope unfurls like a gentle bloom,
Bright in the depths, dispelling gloom.

Faint glimmers in the darkest hour,
Reminders of life's hidden power.
Each flicker soft, a guiding hand,
Luminous shadows, a brighter land.

In the midst of trials and fears,
Hope whispers sweetly, calms our tears.
With every heartbeat, it does grow,
In the dance of life, we glow.

Paths illuminated by faith's embrace,
A journey taken at our own pace.
Through tangled roots and winding trails,
Luminous hope in the wind prevails.

So let us treasure the light we find,
In the shadows, our hearts aligned.
Through every dark, the heart will cope,
In the luminous shadows of hope.

A Flicker in the Dusk

As the sun bows to the night,
A flicker stirs, igniting light.
In the hush of fading day,
Dreams awaken, come what may.

Golden hues turn into gray,
Yet within, the embers play.
Every heartbeat whispers near,
A flicker bright, a flame of cheer.

In the stillness, a spark ignites,
Carving pathways through the heights.
With every breath, it finds its place,
A dance of shadows, a gentle grace.

Through the veils of twilight's shroud,
Hope emerges, strong and proud.
In the echoes of the past,
A flicker shines, love's contrast.

As day surrenders to the gray,
Let that flicker lead the way.
In the dusk where dreams combust,
A beacon bright, in hope we trust.

Illumined by Absence

In silence lingers a hollow space,
Echoes tremble, time's embrace.
Memories linger, bittersweet,
In absence, love finds its beat.

Stars twinkle in the endless night,
Each one a story, a silent light.
Through the void, we navigate,
Illumined by what we create.

Visions arise from a tender past,
In every heartbeat, shadows cast.
Finding solace in what we miss,
In absence, a lingering kiss.

With every tear, we learn to grow,
Through loss, the heart will glow.
Illumined paths, forever bright,
Guided softly by love's light.

Let us cherish what remains,
The whispers of love in our veins.
In absentia, we come to see,
Beauty in moments, eternally.

Ethereal Echo of Yearning

In shadows deep where whispers play,
A longing song begins to sway.
Echoes of dreams both far and near,
Call out softly, melt the fear.

Through twilight's veil, the heart speaks clear,
Every pulse a memory dear.
With every breath, the silence breaks,
Awakening love that never forsakes.

In the mist, where wishes blend,
A gentle breeze our souls commend.
Holding the fragments of what was lost,
In the realm of hearts, there is no cost.

Stars aligned in heavenly grace,
Guide me to that sacred place.
Where echoes dwell, forever bound,
In timeless love, our spirits found.

Let me wander through moonlit nights,
Chasing shadows, chasing lights.
In every echo, I feel the pull,
Yearning whispers, eternally full.

Glimmers of What Could Be

In the dawn, where dreams collide,
Hope like morning starts to glide.
Glimmers shining, bright and bold,
Tales of futures yet untold.

Every heartbeat whispers fate,
Painting visions, never late.
With every step, the path unfolds,
Crafting stories, life's true gold.

Softly beckoning, the road ahead,
Guided by the dreams we've bred.
In the twilight's gentle glow,
What could be begins to grow.

In the silence, futures breathe,
Hope ignites, and doubts bequeath.
With every glimmer, courage swells,
In the heart, possibility dwells.

Together we shall chase the dawn,
Beneath the sky, we'll carry on.
With glimmers bright, we'll forge our way,
Crafting dreams in the light of day.

Light Beyond the Veil

In shadows cast by doubts of night,
A flame awakens, pure and bright.
Beyond the veil, the light shall rise,
Dispelling fears, igniting skies.

Through fabric woven of dreams and hope,
We find a way, we learn to cope.
With every shimmer, darkness fades,
As warmth of light your path invades.

In silence deep, shadows recede,
Truth emerges, planting seed.
Light spills forth, a golden stream,
Illuminating every dream.

Beyond the veil, where visions soar,
Hearts entwine as spirits explore.
Step into the brilliance uncontained,
In love's embrace, we are sustained.

With every glimmer, shadows yield,
In radiant light, our fate is sealed.
Hand in hand, through life we sail,
Together strong, beyond the veil.

Warmth of Distant Embrace

In the twilight, warmth of dreams,
Fills the air with tender beams.
From afar, a gentle call,
Embracing hearts, uniting all.

Through time and space, love's tethered thread,
Brings comfort where our souls have led.
In distant lands, our spirits blend,
Finding strength as we transcend.

With every thought, I feel you near,
In silent echoes, calm my fear.
The warmth of love, a steady glow,
Guides me where the heart shall go.

In every moment, long or brief,
Your presence sheds a bright belief.
In the stillness of the night,
Distant embrace feels so right.

Together woven, our souls align,
In the cosmic dance, our hearts entwine.
With every heartbeat, we embrace,
The warmth of love in distant space.

Wistful Breezes of Desire

In whispers soft, the breezes sigh,
Carrying dreams that float on high.
Each breath a longing, tender, sweet,
Awakens hope where shadows meet.

Stars glimmer faintly in the night,
Guiding hearts toward the light.
A dance of wishes in the air,
Drawing souls, a sacred pair.

Through golden fields, the memories roam,
In every corner, they find a home.
The scent of blossoms lost in time,
Echoes softly, a silent rhyme.

The sunset paints with hues of gold,
A tapestry of stories told.
With each moment, the longing grows,
A wistful breeze that gently blows.

In quiet corners, dreams take flight,
Embracing hope beneath the night.
The world is vast, yet close we feel,
Wistful breezes, our hearts reveal.

Blossoms of Sunset Longing

As daylight fades, the colors blend,
A fleeting moment, a soft ascend.
Petals whisper secrets in the breeze,
Time dances lightly among the trees.

The horizon blushes with tender grace,
In twilight's arms, we find our place.
Each flower a memory, fragrant, bold,
Stories of love and longing told.

Glimmers of hope in the fading light,
Awakening dreams to take flight.
With every stroke, the heavens sigh,
In shimmering hues, the moments lie.

Crimson skies cradle our desires,
Filling our hearts with gentle fires.
The touch of dusk, a lover's caress,
In blossoms' blush, we find our rest.

As stars emerge in twilight's hue,
Longing unfolds; a dream come true.
In every petal, a wish set free,
Blossoms of sunset, you're home to me.

Ripples of Distant Affection

Across the waves, the echoes grow,
Ripples of love both fast and slow.
In distant shores, our hearts connect,
A bond unbroken, deep respect.

Moonlit waters, shimmering bright,
Reflect the dreams we share each night.
Though miles apart, we pull as one,
A dance of souls till day is done.

The breeze carries whispers from afar,
Guiding our hearts like a shining star.
With every tide, our wishes rise,
In the ocean's heart, no goodbyes.

Even as time can stretch and fade,
Our love persists, it won't be swayed.
In quiet moments, we feel the pull,
Ripples of affection, always full.

Together we stand at the edge of dreams,
Listening close to the water's themes.
In every ripple, a sweet embrace,
Distant affection, our sacred space.

Horizons of Heartfelt Longing

Beyond the hills, where shadows play,
Horizons beckon at the end of day.
With every sunset, hopes arise,
Painting the world with heartfelt ties.

In fields of gold, our dreams take form,
A gentle breeze, a tender warm.
As night descends, the stars ignite,
Guiding us softly through the night.

Every glance a promise, unspoken,
In the silence, hearts remain awoken.
Our spirits soar, forever free,
Horizons stretch, just you and me.

Through whispered winds, our secrets flow,
In twilight hours, our feelings grow.
With open arms, the moonlight calls,
Beneath the heavens, our longing sprawls.

In every heartbeat, we hear the song,
Of finding where we both belong.
As dawn breaks gently, love will find,
Horizons of longing, intertwined.

Shimmers of a Forgotten Touch

In the stillness of the night,
Whispers of love softly sing,
Memories linger like starlight,
Carried on the breeze of spring.

Fingers trace the ghostly path,
Where warmth once held me so tight,
Now I walk with shadows' wrath,
Searching for that lost delight.

Reflections dance in the dim light,
Echoes of laughter long gone,
Soft glimmers fade from my sight,
Yet the pulse of dreams lives on.

Waves crash on the shore of time,
Erasing footprints of the past,
In the silence, a quiet rhyme,
Promises made, but none could last.

Yet in the heart's hidden fold,
The shimmer of hope starts to grow,
In every story left untold,
A flicker of warmth, a soft glow.

Glints of Hope on a Distant Horizon

In the dawn's early embrace,
The world awakens anew,
Sunlight paints a gentle face,
Breaking through the morning dew.

Far beyond where dreams take flight,
A glimmer beckons my soul,
Guiding with its tender light,
Toward a vast, uncharted goal.

Each step forward, a whispered prayer,
Winds of change stir in the air,
Through shadows thick, I find my way,
Holding on to hope's bouquet.

Mountains high and valleys low,
All the paths I dare to tread,
With every heartbeat, I will grow,
Chasing the visions in my head.

So let the stars illuminate
The path that I am meant to roam,
For in each glint, I'll cultivate
The strength to make this world my home.

Soft Sparks in the Darkness

When the night wraps its cold hands,
And shadows play their cruel game,
A flicker of warmth understands,
That light resides within the flame.

In the corners of empty rooms,
Hope whispers with a gentle sigh,
Blooming in the heart's dark blooms,
Soft sparks that never say goodbye.

With every tear that paints the ground,
A spark ignites, defies the rain,
In silence, strength can still be found,
Through the sorrow, I will gain.

Though darkness tries to steal my voice,
I rise, I dance in the abyss,
Each spark a reason, each spark a choice,
A flicker of light, a tender kiss.

So let the night be deeply still,
I will embrace the stars above,
With every spark, I build my will,
To forge my path with endless love.

Moonlit Longings Unfulfilled

Beneath the glow of golden beams,
I stand in silence, lost in thought,
The moon spills forth its silver dreams,
A tapestry of wishes sought.

Yet longing hangs like morning mist,
In the shadows, hope feels so near,
Softly sighing, my heart's a tryst,
With echoes of a love sincere.

In night's embrace, I chase the stars,
Through whispered winds that bring me calm,
Though distance feels like endless bars,
I cradle memories like a balm.

Each moment drips like dew from leaves,
A fleeting touch, a breath away,
My heart, a compass that believes,
In the dawn that will break the gray.

So here I stand, with dreams confided,
Wrapped in hopes that never fade,
In the moonlight, love is abided,
Through longings held, a serenade.

Echoes of a Flickering Flame

In shadows deep, a whisper calls,
A dance of light, where darkness falls.
The ember glows, a fleeting sight,
A flicker warms the cold of night.

Soft murmurs pass, of times long gone,
A heart once bold, now weary, drawn.
Yet in the flicker, hope does cling,
And from the ashes, life can spring.

The flame it sways, like thoughts in flight,
A fleeting spark, in endless night.
To chase the shadows, brave the chill,
With every flicker, find the will.

Resilient heart, though battered, torn,
In every flicker, strength is born.
For even small, the flame can rise,
A beacon bright, beneath the skies.

So heed the echoes, let them guide,
Through darkened paths, with hope as pride.
In every flicker, find your way,
And keep the flame alive each day.

Glimmers of the Heart's Desire

In quiet moments, dreams take flight,
Soft whispers spark in the gentle night.
A silver thread, a glimmer rare,
Light's tender touch, a love laid bare.

With every beat, the heart will dance,
In fleeting glimmers, a second glance.
Desires rise, like stars above,
In shadows cast, they weave and shove.

Each hope a petal, fragile, bright,
In gardens lush, they crave the light.
With every sigh, a wish reborn,
In glimmers sweet, hearts are worn.

Through trials faced, the spirit bends,
Yet every loss, the heart transcends.
For in each spark, the soul's own fire,
Awakens bold, the heart's true desire.

So seek the glimmers, hold them near,
In every cherished moment, dear.
With every pulse, let passion play,
In glimmers bright, we find our way.

Ribbons of Light in the Darkness

A tapestry of dreams unfolds,
In ribbons bright, where night beholds.
Threads of light twist through the gray,
A promise whispered, come what may.

Through veils of shadow, hope will weave,
In every heart, a chance to believe.
The darkness fades, a soft embrace,
With ribbons of light, we find our place.

Each flicker sways like gentle waves,
In silent seas, where courage saves.
As whispers rise, and shadows flee,
Ribbons of hope, set spirits free.

With every dawn, new colors blend,
A palette vast, as hearts transcend.
In ribbons bright, our dreams ignite,
Guiding us through the darkest night.

So gather strength, from light's own thread,
In every moment, love is spread.
With ribbons woven, let us sing,
Through darkness deep, our spirits ring.

Remnants of Starlight Yearning

In quiet nights, the stars do weep,
Their distant songs, a longing deep.
Each twinkle tells of dreams once dreamed,
In remnants fond, the heart is schemed.

Soft whispers float on cosmic tides,
While time and space, in silence bides.
For every wish, a tale of light,
In starlit skies, we seek the bright.

Yearning hearts reach through the void,
In every moment, joy deployed.
For remnants lost, we seek and find,
The echoes true, of souls entwined.

A shimmer here, a glimmer there,
In every pulse, we breathe the air.
With every breath, the stars align,
In remnants sweet, our hearts entwine.

So chase the shadows, let them know,
In starlight's arms, the dreams will grow.
For every yearning, love will stay,
In remnants bright, our hopes will play.

Flickering Stars of Memories Past

In the night sky, stars still gleam,
Whispers of dreams like a flowing stream.
Each flicker a tale, a moment caught,
Echoes of laughter, the warmth we sought.

Fading yet bright, the past won't fade,
In shadows of time, sweet memories laid.
We cherish the glow, the spark of the night,
Guiding our hearts through the soft twilight.

Every star holds a fragment of you,
Stories untold, in the dark they strew.
The cosmos alive with love and delight,
As we weave through the fabric of night.

Though years may pass, and moments grow old,
The flickering stars are treasures untold.
In silence they speak, in brightness they laugh,
Illuminating the path of our past.

So let us remember the light that we shared,
The flickering stars for which we had cared.
In the canvas of time, forever they shine,
These flickering stars will always be mine.

Soft Radiance of Unspoken Words

In the hush of the night, words start to dance,
Whispers of thoughts, they beckon a chance.
The unsaid emotions wrapped tenderly tight,
Illuminate dreams in the softest of light.

Every glance shared speaks louder than song,
Binding our hearts where we both belong.
Silences filled with the glowing delight,
A radiance soft, in shadows of night.

Tender moments linger, like sweet summer rain,
Carving our souls, yet never in vain.
Soft radiance whispers, on the edge of our sight,
Unspoken words that encompass our light.

In the depth of the quiet, the truth we confess,
The beauty of silence, our hearts still impress.
Like stars in the evening, they shimmer and glow,
Unveiling the feelings we long to bestow.

Let us cherish the tales that our eyes have confided,
In the softest of moments, our hearts are divided.
A warmth that reminds us, we're never alone,
In the radiance of love, we each find our home.

Chasing the Light of Yesterday

Underneath the vast, glowing skies,
We chase the echoes where time softly lies.
Moments once held in the grasp of our hands,
Now linger like footprints washed from the sands.

With each fleeting hour, we seek what we lost,
Braving the shadows, no matter the cost.
Chasing the light that we knew long ago,
We dance through the memories, a bittersweet flow.

Faded photographs whisper our names,
In the dance of the past, we play ancient games.
As dawn begins breaking, we reach for the glow,
Chasing the light with the hearts we bestow.

The echoes of laughter, a sweet serenade,
Illuminating paths where our dreams were laid.
As time passes slowly, we strive to hold tight,
To the moments of joy that once filled our sight.

So here we stand, in the glow of today,
Chasing the light of the past, come what may.
For in every heartbeat, every soft sigh,
Lives the light of yesterday, never to die.

Gleams of Hearts Apart

In the distance, I see your light shine bright,
Sparkling like diamonds, my heart takes flight.
Though miles may stretch and worlds may divide,
The gleams of our hearts hold love deep inside.

Whispers of hope in the silence we share,
Threads of connection that float in the air.
In the tapestry woven with memories sweet,
Gleams of our love make us whole, incomplete.

The laughter we've shared still dances in rays,
Guiding my soul through the longest of days.
Each gleam like a sunbeam that warms the cold night,
Reminds me of you in the soft glowing light.

As shadows may fall, and storms may arise,
Our hearts remain anchored, no need for disguise.
For gleams of our spirits still shimmer and play,
Uniting the fragments that make us today.

Though time may lead us down different paths,
The gleams of our hearts remind us of laughs.
In the quilt of existence, we both have a part,
Forever entwined, with gleams of the heart.

Secrets in the Softest Nocturne

Whispers ride the evening breeze,
Stars are cloaked in ancient tales.
Shadows dance among the trees,
Each leaf carries night's soft veils.

Underneath the velvet sky,
Silent hearts begin to dream.
Echoes of a lullaby,
Moonlit paths that softly gleam.

In the stillness find your peace,
Glimmers of a world unseen.
Secrets that the dark releases,
Cradled in the night's sweet sheen.

Gentle whispers, tender sighs,
Lost within the velvet dark.
Shooting stars, they swiftly fly,
Leaving trails, a haunting mark.

Embrace the magic of the night,
Let it guide your weary soul.
In the shadows, find your light,
In the stillness, you are whole.

Reflections in the Moonlight Pool

Glimmers dance on water's face,
Echoes of a past so bright.
Rippling dreams in a gentle space,
Chasing shadows in the light.

Each wave tells a whispered lore,
Carried tales of time gone by.
Beneath the surface, treasures store,
Hidden secrets deep and shy.

Moonlight casts a silver thread,
Binding past and present's gleam.
In the silence, words unsaid,
Flow like currents in a dream.

Wishing stones are tossed with grace,
Hopes and wishes intertwined.
Find your truth in this safe place,
In the water's depth, you'll find.

Every glance, a story spun,
Between the waves, a captured breath.
Reflections speak where dreams are won,
In the moonlight, life and death.

Flickering Candle of the Heart

In the silence, embers glow,
Softly lighting paths unknown.
Casts a warmth in shadows low,
Kindling dreams that feel like home.

With each flicker, hope ignites,
Guiding souls through darkest nights.
In its flame, a dance of light,
Breath of love, in tender sights.

Through the trials, it remains,
A beacon in the stormy skies.
Through the laughter, through the pains,
Its steadfast glow never dies.

Hand in hand, the light we share,
Casting beams on paths we tread.
In the flicker, find your prayer,
Voices lifted, hearts are fed.

Let it shine, a guiding star,
In the night, a loyal friend.
Though the world may seem afar,
Candle's warmth, love shall extend.

Beacons of Unquenchable Hope

In the distance, candles gleam,
A constellation born of fire.
Through the chaos, hold the dream,
Each flame a spark of pure desire.

Mountains loom, but hearts won't break,
For the light will guide the way.
With each step, the brave will take,
Unquenchable in night and day.

With every trial we endure,
Hope will rise like morning sun.
A light that's steadfast, strong, and pure,
Beacons bright till battles won.

In the whispers of the night,
Dreamers gather, souls entwined.
Together, hearts ignite the light,
Shadows fade, and peace we find.

Stand united, spirits soar,
In the face of all despair.
With every flicker, brighter roar,
Hope shines forth, a love laid bare.

Flickers of Unattainable Dreams

In twilight's glow, we chase the light,
Illusions dance, just out of sight.
The whispers call, yet fade away,
Fleeting visions of yesterday.

Stars align like scattered seeds,
Growing hopes that time concedes.
Fragments flicker, tepid flames,
Chasing shadows, calling names.

The heart's desire, an endless quest,
Ever striving, never rest.
In the silence, echoes scream,
Tangled webs of each lost dream.

Yet in the night, the fire glows,
A spark survives where no one knows.
With whispered prayers, we dare to yearn,
For the flickers, we still discern.

So hold the light, embrace the chase,
With every step, there's hope to trace.
In shadows deep, our spirits gleam,
For we are born from unattainable dreams.

Shades of Sweet Nostalgia

Softly falls the autumn leaf,
A reminder, sweet yet brief.
Memories linger in every hue,
Shades of longing, shades of you.

Windows open to skies of gray,
Whispers of what kept at bay.
Echoes play in the quiet room,
Wrap me tight in their gentle bloom.

Time flows like a trickling stream,
Capturing whispers, savored dream.
The laughter lingers in the air,
Lost in moments, beyond compare.

With every glance, my heart will dance,
In your smile, I find my chance.
Though seasons change and days move on,
In shades of sweet, my heart stays strong.

So raise a glass to years gone by,
To moments we can't let die.
In nostalgia's arms, we will remain,
Forever wrapped in joy and pain.

A Flame Across the Ocean

Across the waves, a fire glows,
A beacon bright where the sea wind blows.
Hearts afloat on tides unknown,
In distant lands, love has grown.

The horizon sings of hopes untold,
A story written, brave and bold.
In the midnight sky, a spark ignites,
Uniting souls on starry nights.

Though miles apart, the heart beats true,
In every whisper, it calls to you.
With every dawn, our spirits soar,
A flame that binds, forevermore.

In ships of dreams, we sail afar,
Navigating by a guiding star.
For love transcends the darkest tides,
A flame that never, ever hides.

So let the fire light our way,
Across the ocean, come what may.
With steadfast hope, we find our way,
A flame that vows to never sway.

Lullabies of the Unseen

In the hush of night, a song takes flight,
Whispers of dreams weave soft and light.
In shadows deep, the heart takes heed,
Lullabies of what we need.

Stars above twinkle with care,
Carrying hopes laid bare.
Each note cradles the silent sighs,
A gentle cradle for weary eyes.

The world slows down, the moments pause,
Wrapped in magic without cause.
In the arms of quiet grace,
Lullabies our thoughts embrace.

Echoes linger, a soft refrain,
Tales of joy, tales of pain.
Through the stillness, dreams take flight,
In the lull of the velvet night.

So close your eyes, let shadows lead,
To the unheard, where hearts are freed.
In the beauty of what's unseen,
Find your peace, soft and serene.

www.ingramcontent.com/pod-product-compliance
Ingram Content Group UK Ltd.
Pitfield, Milton Keynes, MK11 3LW, UK
UKHW020054171224
452675UK00013B/1106

9 789908 150000